HOW TO PLAY DRUMS

Vincent L. Mott

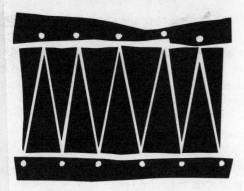

A **MAESTRO** Publication

ISBN: 0 8494 1550 0

85-10

Contents

INTRODUCTION

The Art Of Drumming

The art of drumming may be described as the development of basic, or rudimental, "stroke" and "tap" patterns. These patterns may be simple, or they may be combinations of two or more patterns combined to form a more complex pattern. In the interests of simplicity and for the purpose of learning more about drumming, the art has been reduced to twenty six patterns of a basic nature. These twenty six patterns are the rudiments of drumming.

If one develops the twenty six rudiments to a high degree of proficiency, he will have at his command every possible rhythmic figure he is likely to encounter as a drummer. Regardless of the apparent complexity of a rhythmic pattern, a trained drummer can recognize a rudimental pattern, or a part of a rudiment. Just as a scale can be recognized from a fragment of a scale, or from an ascending or descending part of a scale, so too, can the drum rudiment be recognized, even when interlaced with others.

The popularity of drums goes back to ancient civilizations. There are monuments and inscriptions in Egypt, Assyria and Persia, depicting drums of various sizes and shapes. Several thousand years before Christianity, the Chinese Tom Tom was brought to India where Buddhist Priests introduced them into their religious services. Large and small Tom Toms later appeared in Turkey, Greece and Rome, and found their way into western Europe. In Basle, Switzerland, each year thousands of drummers participate in a gigantic celebration similar to our Mardi Gras held in New Orleans.

Columbus found drums used by natives of San Salvador, and on the Isle of Hispanola, now known as Haiti and the Dominican Republic. This writer visited these countries and found their Voodoo drumming so exciting, he returned to do some serious research. The native drummers were most cooperative and eager to play. Once shown a technical display, it was amazing how quickly they learned to execute intricate stick work. They do the Single Stroke Roll remarkably well, and with machine-like precision, and when they gather for a ritual, their rhythms become exceedingly complicated.

Human beings everywhere have always been fascinated by drums. The drum was probably man's first musical instrument. Even today, there are many lands where no other musical instrument is to be found, and where drums are used in religious rituals, for transmitting signals, and as a background for native dancing. Among the Batela, Bantu and Sudanese tribes in the Belgian Congo, a well developed system of communication by means of drums, has been evolved. Every civilization and every culture uses drums in one form or another.

Primitive drums were any hollow objects that could emit a booming sound when struck. Hollow logs made very effective predecessors of drums. Being wooden, they had remarkably large carrying power, surpassing that of drum heads of skins. The word drum appeared in England about the middle of the sixteenth century, to describe an instrument consisting of a hollow cylinder with a membrane tightly covering each end, which was beaten with sticks or the fingers. It also describes objects resembling a drum in shape. The term is also applied to large circular masses of stone still standing in Selinus, Sicily. They are eight to ten feet in diameter and about six feet high. Sicilians call them the Drums of Selinus.

The threadbare pun "we were all born with drums in our ears" is, in fact, an expression of the universal appeal of drums. In our own civilization, concert bands, symphony orchestras and dance bands owe much of their appeal to the drums which punctuate the music and add life and sparkle.

The word method has been used before in titles of books. It is supposed to mean a special way of instruction. There are "methods" of studying to play the piano and other instruments. However, the authors seldom laid claim to a method. Their pupils did it for them, and once it was accepted, it stayed that way.

"Methods" have been claimed for drum books, too. The eastern section of the United States accepted the Strube Method, which was adopted by the United States Army in 1869. The middle West, the West and parts of the south retained the Bruce Method, which had been adopted earlier, in 1862. Both methods were practically identical, each having twenty one rudiments from Charles Ashworth's book, published in 1812. Bruce made some additions and showed thirty eight rudiments. Strube, no doubt, had the twenty six letters of the alphabet in mind, used twenty six rudiments, and added a few exercises.

In 1933, the National Association of Rudimental Drummers was organized in Chicago by William F. Ludwig, Sr. during the American Legion Convention. The original membership consisted of thirteen drummers. Like the thirteen stripes on the American Flag, they commemorate the event by requiring thirteen rudiments to pass their examinations. This organization has helped improve the art of drumming throughout the world, by encouraging greater interest in the rudiments of drumming.

The drum student should realize at the outset that in addition to acquiring drum technique, he is to develop good musicianship, which is merely good taste, good judgement, and good musical manners. This trait will be developed properly and beneficially, if he keeps good drum company and realizes that the drumming of all leading performers is always clean, distinct and exact. It is never careless or indistinct, nor is it weak when it should be bold nor boisterious when it should be subdued.

If the student has a flair for drumming he has a valuable advantage. But talent alone does not guarantee success. Industriousness and practice are still required, for one learns only by doing. It is therefore appropriate to tell the student that he need not be disturbed if he does not have great talent, because his rhythmical bump can be cultivated by systematic and regular practice. This, coupled with a knowledge of the twenty six rudiments and their applications, is the formula for success.

THE ELEMENTS OF MUSICAL NOTATION

Musical notation is written the same world over. In order to facilitate reading (and writing) musical notation, a beginner starts out with a symbol that designates one "beat." In this sense, the word beat refers to a definite period of time. If we want to "explain" the regular recurrence of single beats, we could simply count them off very regularly by saying one two, three, four one, two, three, four; one, two, etc. If the rhythm felt like a waltz, UM, pah, pah, UM, pah, pah, in which a heavy beat (accent) falls regularly on the FIRST beat of three, (on the UM, not on the pah, pah), we would say ONE, two, three, ONE, two, three, etc.

In musical notation, one accented beat followed by an unaccented beat is written by solid black notes as follows:

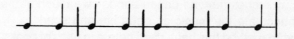

These solid black notes are called quarter-notes. Each received ONE beat.

A quarter-note ♩, is solid black with a straight stem. The stem may be written going up ♩, or going down. ♩

Of course, there are times when we need notes that are longer or shorter than a single beat. We will also want symbols for periods of silence instead of for sounds. Symbols for silence are called rests. They have definite values just as notes have their own definite values.

The quarter-rest is 𝄽 , and equals a quarter-note, ♩ .

Two quarter-notes, of course, are equal to a half-note, ♩♩ = ♩

The half-rest is a hat right side up, ▬, like a solid block on top of a line, ♩♩ = ♩ = ▬

Two half-notes are equal to one whole-note, ♩♩ = 𝅝

The whole-rest is a hat upside down, like a solid block hanging under the line, ▬

A quarter-note also equals two eighth-notes, ♩ = ♪♪

Single eighth-notes are written with a single flag hung on the quarter-note, but are also written connected together by a single heavy line,

♪ ♪ ♪ ♪   ♪ ♪   ♫♫   ♫

The eighth-rest is simply a single flag hanging from a slanted pole:

$$♪ \quad = \quad ʔ$$

eighth note equals eighth rest

These few symbols will suffice for the present. As the student progresses with these, others will become practically self explanatory. The following chart, however, may be found useful.

◄ One inch ►					
Whole Note	Half Notes	Quarter Notes	Eighth Notes	Sixteenth Notes	Thirty-second Notes
𝅝	𝅗𝅥 𝅗𝅥	♩ ♩ ♩ ♩	♫♫♫ ♫♫	♬♬♩♩	♬♪♪♩
▬	▬	𝄽	ʔ	⁊	⁊
Whole Rest	Half Rest	Quarter Rest	Eighth Rest	Sixteenth Rest	Thirty-second Rest

Drum music is usually written on a musical staff like music for melodic instruments.

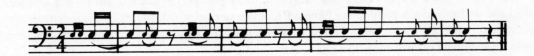

Drum music written on a staff.

Since drum music does not involve changes of pitch, it may also be written on a single line. We shall write our drum music (for the most part), on a single line, as in the following example:

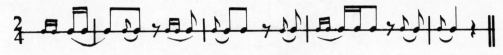

Drum music written on a single line.

In a March, we feel a repetition of an accented beat followed by an unaccented beat, repeated over and over again. It is written and explained by counting:

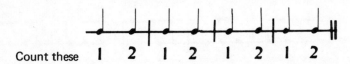

Count these   1   2   1   2   1   2   1   2

In this example we realize that the music is divided into uniform groups of two beats each. A group of two beats is followed by another group of two beats, over and over again. These groups are called measures. And so, in this March the music is divided into measures of two beats each, with a quarter-note getting one beat. That means that each measure will contain two quarter-notes or their equivalent. To make this perfectly clear at a glance, musicians use symbols for various time-signatures, which they place at the beginning of a composition.

In the case of this March, the time-signature is the fraction $\frac{2}{4}$. It tells us at a glance:

IN THIS PIECE, THERE WILL BE TWO BEATS TO A MEASURE; EACH BEAT WILL BE DESIGNATED BY A QUARTER-NOTE OR ITS EQUIVALENT.

Expressed properly in musical notation, the above march is

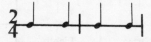

In a Waltz, the feeling is for three beats to a measure, with an accent on the first beat. It is therefore properly notated and counted:

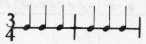

In $\frac{3}{4}$ "time" (meter is the proper word), the time-signature tells us at a glance that the music is divided into measures of *three* beats each, that the quarter-note gets one beat, and that there will be three quarter-notes, or their equivalent, in each measure.

Of course, there are other time-signatures for other meters, but the student should first learn to read and understand the preliminary Simple Reading Exercises which follow by playing them with the hands on a table in front of him. This will furnish exceedingly valuable practice in reading, and will help speed him on his way.

Be sure to count out loud during all practice periods. This is one of the most important musical habits to acquire during the initial period of study. If you can say it, you can play it.

READING EXERCISES

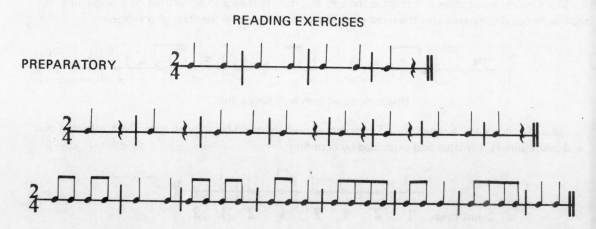

PREPARATORY

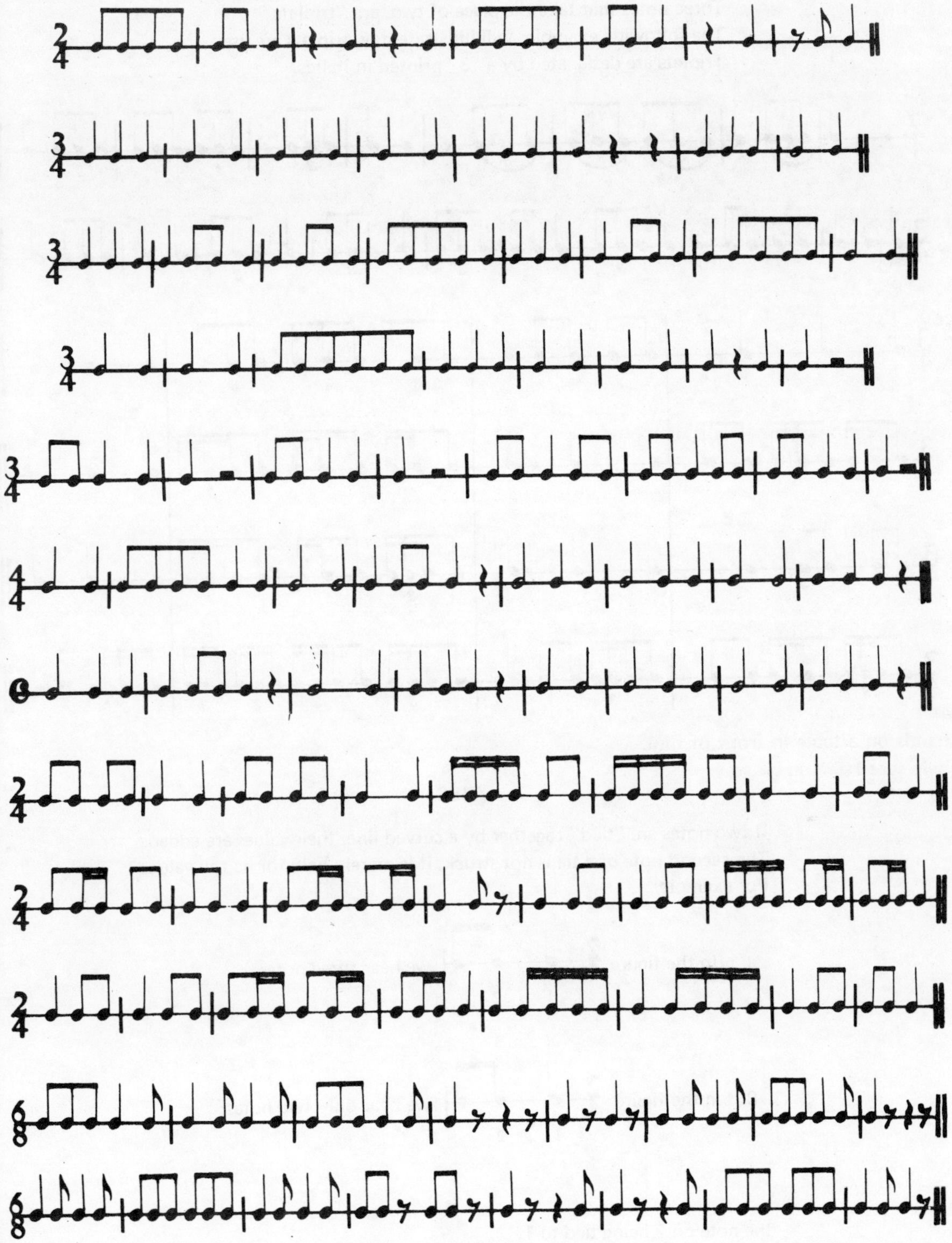

TRIPLETS:

Three notes that take the place of two, are "triplets."
The following examples will illustrate how triplets are used.
Triplets are designated by a "3" printed in italics.

TIES:

If two notes are "tied" together by a curved line, their values are added.
The second note of a tie is not struck, it is merely held for its full value.
For example:

In the figure  we hear three notes;

But in the figure  we hear only two notes,

the note on 2 being tied to 1.

The following studies will illustrate.

DOTTED NOTES:

A dot added to a note, adds half of the note's value to that note. For example, the following exercises show how a dotted note is like two tied notes, in which the dot is substituted for the tied note:

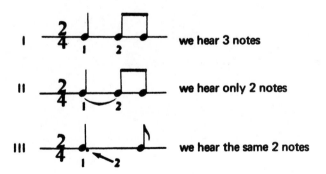

Notice that II and III sound exactly alike. The dot always belongs to the next beat. In the above example it is equal to an eighth note because it is attached to a quarter-note, (i.e., half the note's value). The dot and the eigth-note constitute the second beat in the measure. The dot is counted "2"; the eighth-note is counted "&."

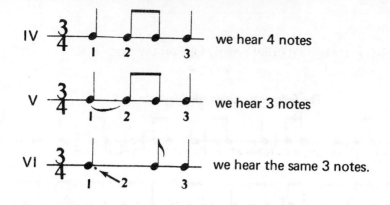

IV — we hear 4 notes

V — we hear 3 notes

VI — we hear the same 3 notes.

Notice that V and VI sound exactly alike. The explanation here is the same as for II and III. The figure shown in VI is the pattern of "Silent Night":

Here is the rhythmic pattern of "Santa Lucia":

10

In $\frac{2}{4}$ meter, a natural accent falls on the first beat.

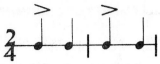

In $\frac{3}{4}$ meter, a natural accent falls on the first beat.

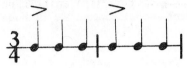

In $\frac{4}{4}$ meter, a natural accent falls on the first and third beat.

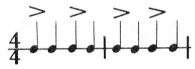

In $\frac{6}{8}$ meter, a natural accent falls on the first and fourth beat.

The (naturally) accented beats are called down beats, the (naturally) unaccented beats are the up beats. Very often a composition starts on an unaccented beat. The first "measure" of such a composition is therefore not a complete measure, but whatever is lacking in it will be found in the last measure of the composition.

The Star Spangled Banner starts on an up beat in $\frac{3}{4}$ meter. It starts on the 3rd beat.

THE ELEMENTS OF DRUMMING

In drumming we employ the arm, the wrist, the hand and the fingers. We may use the right hand or the left hand, or both. As a drummer it will be necessary to develop an instantly responsive sense of selection. Although everyone will claim he knows his left hand from his right, it is surprising how often the embryo drummer can become confused on this very elementary point. To instill a keen sense of selectivity of hands, the student should concentrate studiously on the first few preliminary exercises.

R stands for Right Hand, L for Left Hand.

The Three R's Of Drumming Are Rhythm, Reverts, Reverses.

Rhythm is a uniform repetition of a beat or accent. Everyone has a sense of rhythm, but it should be exceptionally well developed in drummers.

Reverts means to repeat a figure exactly as it was first executed. Some drummers like to say a figure reverts if it is repeated "the same way, like going on a one-way street, in one direction," i.e., if it started with the Right Hand, it must start again with the Right Hand when repeated.

Reverses means the figure may be played in the "other direction, like going on a two-way street," i.e., if started with the Right Hand, the repetition should be started with the Left Hand.

Facility with the Three Rs is the basic training required of every drummer. When these are grasped the student is well on the road to good drumming.

The right stick is held between the thumb and the second joint of the middle finger, palm down, with the remaining fingers curled over the stick lightly but securely. Hold it as you would hold a knife to cut a cake.

The left stick is held palm up, in the hollow between the thumb and forefinger, the first two fingers curling over the stick. The last two fingers are under the stick, close together with the tips almost straight out, and in position to lift the stick. If these two fingers touch the palm it will cramp your muscles. The stick rests on the third finger which acts as a shelf. Keep both arms, the wrists, and the fingers relaxed at all times.

There are four natural positions of holding the sticks. No matter what you are playing you should be in one of these positions.

THE FOUR NATURAL POSITIONS

STARTING AND ENDING
ALL RUDIMENTS OR DRUM FIGURES

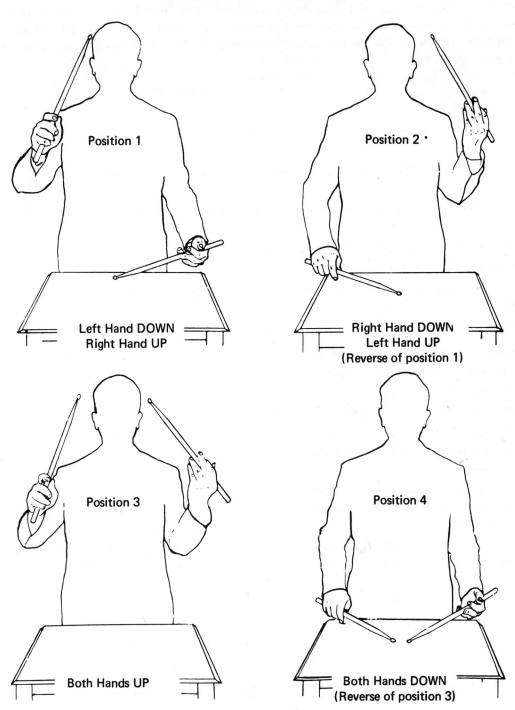

Position 1

**Left Hand DOWN
Right Hand UP**

Position 2 ·

**Right Hand DOWN
Left Hand UP
(Reverse of position 1)**

Position 3

Both Hands UP

Position 4

**Both Hands DOWN
(Reverse of position 3)**

STROKES AND TAPS

Two common motions performed by drummers are Strokes and Taps. A Stroke is an arm and wrist motion. A Tap is a wrist and finger motion. There are 3 Strokes and 2 Taps.

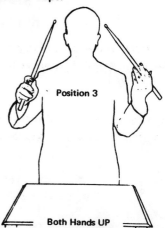

A Full stroke is an arm movement. It starts from Position 3 (both hands up), with force with either hand, and returns to Position 3. A Full Stroke starts and ends in the same position.

A Down Stroke is also an arm movement. It comes from a high hand position, but stays down when completed. It can start from Position 1, 2 or 3, but never from Position 4.

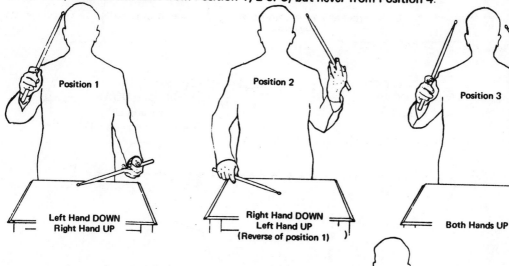

An Up Stroke Always starts from Position 4. Strike the drum while the hand is rising.

A Tap is a wrist and finger motion. It starts and ends in Position 4. It may be a light tap (pianissimo), or a heavy tap (forte).

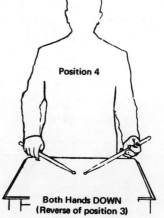

14

PART II

THE TWENTY-SIX RUDIMENTS

INTRODUCTION

A drum tone cannot be prolonged in the same way a singer can hold a long note. A drum tone is an instantaneous "snap." If a singer produced these notes , each would be of different duration.

A long tone is made up of many consecutive sounds of short duration. The ear accepts them as a continuous tone. On a drum, sounds of different duration are produced by means of Rolls, and are written

Bars on the stems of notes may also represent notes to be repeated. For example, a quarter-note with a bar on the stem ♩, is the same as two eighth-notes: ♪♪ A half-note with a single bar on its stem is the same as four eighth-notes: 𝅗𝅥 = ♪♪♪♪

Similarly,

Drumming starts as a series of single right hand strokes:

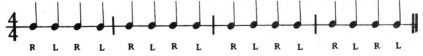

Next comes a series of single left hand strokes:

Practice these two simple exercises with the idea of making them sound exactly alike. At first, the left hand may seem a little weaker. When the single lefts sound the same as the single rights, proceed to the following Singles Hand To Hand:

Practice slowly; strive only for accuracy and evenness; speed will come by itself. The monotony of the first few exercises will not be long, for after a little fluency has been attained, the student will realize that he has made progress. The importance of truly understanding the studies prior to the first rudiment cannot be over emphasized.

These Hand To Hand Singles develop into the Single Stroke Roll, or Tremolo.

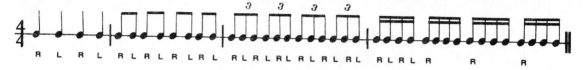

THE SINGLE STROKE
Single Stroke Roll
RUDIMENT A
The First Rudiment

This book is not divided into "lessons." The student may progress at such a rate as will best suit his own capabilities and time. Since the work is arranged progressively, the only precaution to be observed is that the student master each rudiment before proceeding to the next.

Of the three early drum books (Ashworth's, Bruce's and Strube's), it was Strube who described the Single Stroke Roll in 1869. These early books were written by military men for the Army Bands of the United States. In their day it was the rule to commence the rudiments with the left hand. Today, however, with the art of drumming more advanced, we commence the rudiments with the right hand. The marching drummer steps forward with the left foot. As he does so, the drum, suspended as it is, makes an upward motion. It is natural to meet the impact of the first step with the stick of the right hand. The same applies to the next step when the left hand meets the upward motion made by the right step.

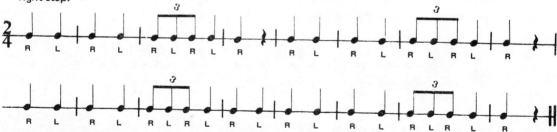

In the above exercise, notice that the right hand leads off in every case on the down-beat, the naturally accented beat. This selection of the right hand as the lead hand has become the modern accepted way of drumming, whether marching or sitting. Keep the right hand as the lead hand, and soon you will instinctively start with your right hand. This procedure was emphasized as far back as 1886 in Sousa's "Trumpet and Drum," page 45, and in J. Moore's "Art of Drumming," pages 20 to 26, (1937).

THE SINGLE STROKE
Single Stroke Roll

The following Single Stroke Rolls are included for reference. They are also known as "Shivers." They may start with either hand. All are accented like the Single Five Stroke.

1. The Single Five Stroke Roll.

2. The Single Seven Stroke Roll.

3. The Single Nine Stroke Roll.

4. The Single Ten Stroke Roll.

5. The Single Thirteen Stroke Roll (triplets or 16ths).

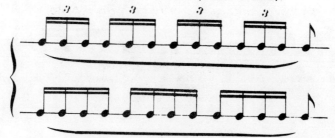

THE DOUBLE STROKE
Double Stroke Roll, Long Roll

RUDIMENT B
The Second Rudiment

The Single Stroke develops into pairs of single strokes, and becomes The Double Stroke.

By doubling hand to hand singles

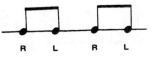

we get hand to hand doubles

First let us take Right Hand Doubles:

The HAND MOTIONS are down -up; down -up; down -up.
Practice these hand motions and say: Down-Up;   Down-Up.

Continue to practice this exercise until you can do it with ease, and with some degree of force.

Left Hand Doubles are done the same way:

Continue to practice this exercise until the LEFT HAND has acquired some facility.

The next step is Hand To Hand Doubles:

(This is also known as the daddy-mammy.)

When it has acquired a fair degree of speed it is the Long Roll, notated

Practice the following exercises for the development of the Long Roll. (Played properly, the effect is that of a locomotive starting slowly and gradually accelerating.)

LONG ROLL

(For better control, practice with and without the accents.)

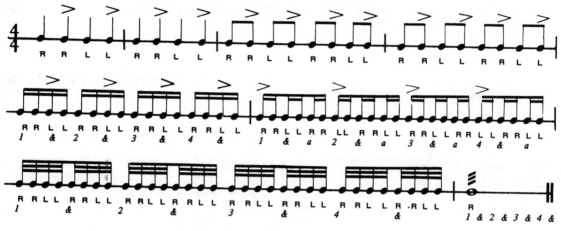

CALIFORNIA CHAMPION

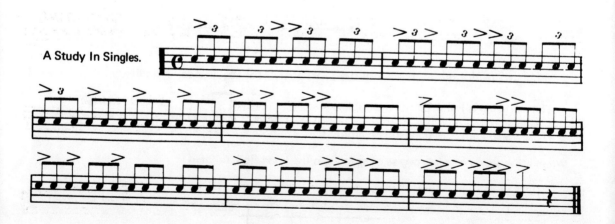

A Study In Singles.

THE DOUBLE STROKE
Double Stroke Roll

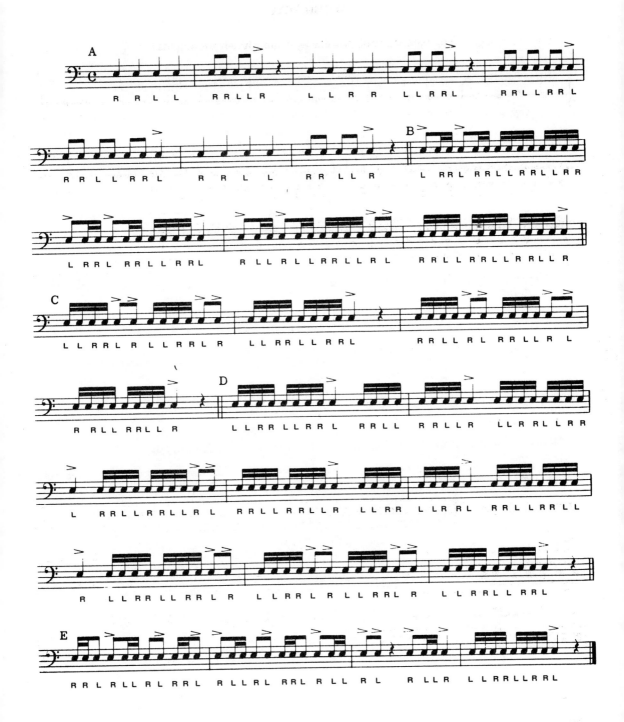

PARADIDDLES
Combinations Of A and B

RUDIMENT C
The Third Rudiment

Combinations of the first two rudiments are called Paradiddles. (Singles plus Doubles give us Paradiddles.)

Three Paradiddles are commonly used. The combinations are practically unlimited.

The Single Paradiddle.

Say: "You can do it, nothing to it."

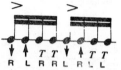

The hand motions are: Down, up, tap, tap. Accent first downstroke of each group.

Notice the pattern of the Single Paradiddle is *one RL* followed by a Double.

The Double Paradiddle.

Say: Dou-ble Par-a-did-dle."

The hand motions are: Down, tap, tap, up, tap, tap. One accent only on the *dou* in "double."

Notice the pattern of the Double Paradiddle is *two RL* followed by a Double.

The Triple Paradiddle.

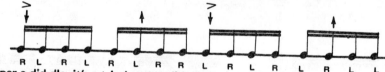

Say: "It's a tri-ple par-a-did-dle, it's a tri-ple par-a-did-dle."

The hand motions are: Down, tap, tap, tap, tap, up, tap, tap.

Notice the pattern of the Triple Paradiddle is *three RL* followed by a Double.

For accuracy use one accent only. In dance work effects, professional drummers often place accents differently, but that does not concern us at present.

COMBINATIONS
Paradiddles

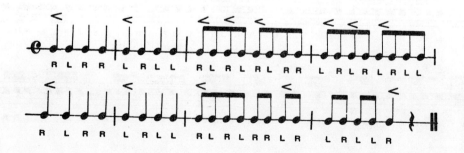

PARADIDDLES
Combinations of Rudiments A & B

23

THE ROLLS GROUP

Eleven commonly accepted rudiments are classified in this category. However, if we include Rudiments A and B, (Single Stroke Roll and Double Stroke Roll) we actually have thirteen rolls.

For the sake of simplicity and a better grasp of the rudiments, it seems more practical to show the development of the Roll Group from the first two simple rudiments, A and B. Note that the third rudiment, Paradiddles, is not one of this group.

In addition to Rudiments A and B, the eleven members of the Roll Group are:

Rudiment D — Single Four Stroke Roll
Rudiment E — Five Stroke Roll
Rudiment F — Six Stroke Roll
Rudiment G — Seven Stroke Roll
Rudiment H — Eight Stroke Roll
Rudiment I — Nine Stroke Roll
Rudiment J — Ten Stroke Roll
Rudiment K — Eleven Stroke Roll
Rudiment L — Thirteen Stroke Roll
Rudiment M — Fifteen Stroke Roll
Rudiment N — Seventeen Stroke Roll

THE SINGLE FOUR STROKE ROLL

RUDIMENT D
The Fourth Rudiment

This rudiment is often called a Four Stroke Ruff, but it is in no way related to the Ruff Group. Its place is logically in the Roll Group since it is descended directly from the Single Stroke Roll, the first rudiment. It starts and ends in Position 4.

It is written

The motions are

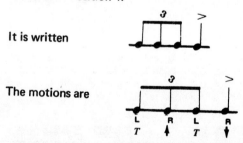

Position 4

Both Hands DOWN
(Reverse of position 3)

Repeat the same way. It sounds like rig-a-ma-jig.

If played fast, they are called Fast Fours, written in 16ths,

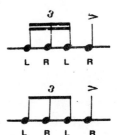

If played slowly, they are called Slow Fours, written in 8ths,

Note the accent on the last note.

    This rudiment appears sufficiently often to be noted in Edward Elgar's *Pomp and Circumstance,* and Anton Dvorak's *New World Symphony.* In Rossini's La Gazza Ladra *(The Thieving Magpie)* it appears as

Played Open

MAESTOSO

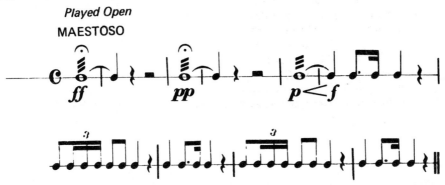

    In Ravel's Bolero, it appears coupled with another rudiment which we shall soon meet (Single Ten Stroke).

Played Open

In Meacham's American Patrol it is written

Played Closed

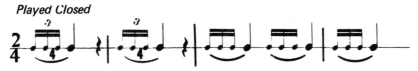

    Ashworth, Bruce and Strube do not mention this rudiment, but it appears in Sousa's book (1886) on page 41. It is mentioned by Haskell Haar, and in Andrew V. Scott's Drumology, page 34. Scott's sticking of this rudiment is similar to that of a Single Drag, which we shall meet later.

SHORT EXERCISES: The Four Stroke Roll.

Tempo Marziale *(from Gounod's FAUST)*

Allegro energico *(from Wagner's RIENZI)*

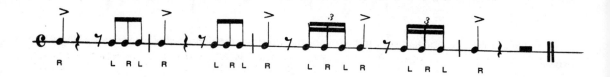

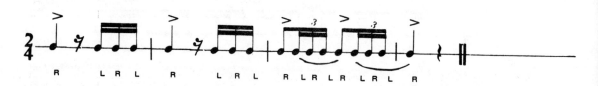

(from Bizet's PATRIE)

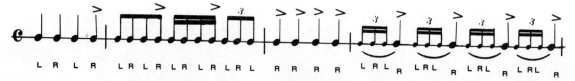

Note: This symbol means "repeat previous measure."

26

THE SINGLE FOUR STROKE ROLL

THE FIVE STROKE ROLL

RUDIMENT E
The Fifth Rudiment

The Five Stroke Roll is a "Gruppeto" of five Strokes consisting of two Doubles and a Single. It starts and ends in Position 3 except when entering another rudiment. The motions should change to conform with the rudiment you are about to play. If it is to be repeated, the Position and motions remain the same.

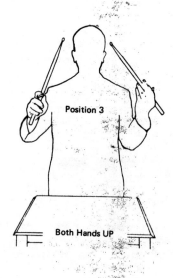

Position 3

Both Hands UP

It is written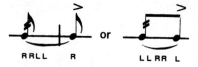

Starting on Up-beat.

Starting on Down-beat.

A group of Fives frequently follows a Single Right Stroke:

The Five Stroke Roll reverses, and is played hand to hand. The Right Hand leads.

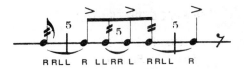

R RLL   R LL RR L   R RLL   R

If only one Five is called for, make it a Right Hand Five.

The Five Stroke Roll often appears as an entrance into other rudiments:

Singles following a Five:

L   R   L   R

Paradiddles and a Single
following a Five:

L   R   R   L   R   L   L   R

When practicing the Five Stroke Roll, say:

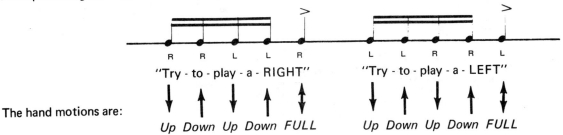

R   R   L   L   R   L   L   R   R   L

"Try - to - play - a - RIGHT"   "Try - to - play - a - LEFT"

The hand motions are:

Up Down Up Down FULL   Up Down Up Down FULL

At the word Full you should be back to starting Position 3. Do not confuse this *Five Stroke* Roll with the *Single Stroke* Five. (Review Rudiment A, Singles) When one speaks of a Five Stroke Roll it is the Double Stroke which is meant.

Practice a Five Stroke Roll going into a Single Paradiddle:

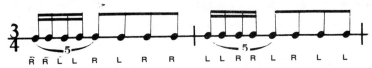

R R L L R   L   R   R   L L R R L   R   L   L

Now practice the Single Stroke Five going into a Single Paradiddle:

R L R L   R   L   R   R   L R L R L   R   L   L

Practice these with the idea of making them *sound alike.*

Ashworth called this rudiment the Mother Roll. Some arrangers write it  and leave it to the discretion of the drummer whether to play a Five or a Seven (another rudiment). If the tempo is fast, use a Five; if slow, a Seven may be used.

Examples of the Five Stroke Roll are found in Pique Dame Overture, Three Camps, Stars and Stripes. John Heney, one of Sousa's drummers, stated it was Sousa himself who asked his drummers to play Five Stroke Rolls preceded by a fast grace note, to be played *one way only,* accented as shown:

Heney further stated it was done for a more effective martial mood. Sousa did not believe in giving away his secrets, but this was one of them. He never showed Five Stroke Rolls printed as such in his music. Sousa preferred them to Sevens, and loved drums and drumming. He cooperated with his drummers, and in return, they performed admirably. This figure can be described as a Flam Five Stroke, but need not concern the student now. It will be more fully appreciated later.

OPENING & CLOSING*
THE FIVE STROKE ROLL

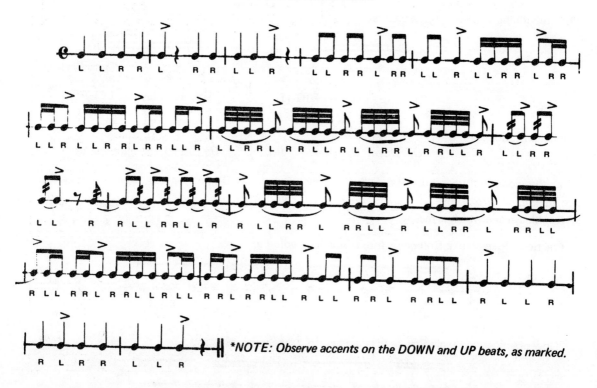

*NOTE: Observe accents on the DOWN and UP beats, as marked.

30

THE FIVE STROKE ROLL

THE SIX STROKE ROLL

RUDIMENT F
The Sixth Rudiment

This rudiment is a Five Stroke with an added Single. It starts and ends in Position 3, both hands up.

It is written:

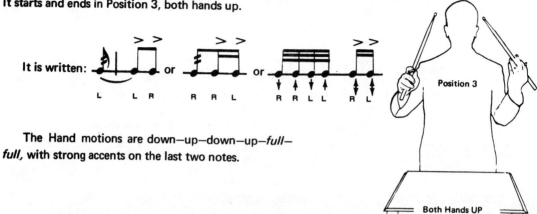

The Hand motions are down—up—down—up—*full*—*full*, with strong accents on the last two notes.

Practice the following and execute the accents very boldly:

Here is an example of 2 Singles, 2 Sixes, and 1 Five:

Here is a Six followed by a bass drum beat, the last measure a Paradiddle left stroke:

This rudiment is not listed by Ashworth, Bruce or Strube. Wilcoxon uses it in his Modern Rudimental Swing Solos:

Unlike Fives, the Six Stroke Roll does not Reverse, but it can be started with either the right or left hand. When Sixes appear in succession, they Revert (same sticking).

ULANO SENT ME

THE SIX STROKE ROLL

34

THE SEVEN STROKE ROLL

RUDIMENT G
The Seventh Rudiment

This rudiment is positively a *must*. It is written:

and is often written this way:

It is also used before Paradiddles:

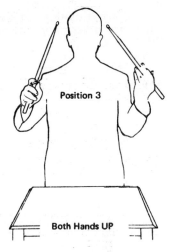

Position 3

Both Hands UP

Seven Stroke Roll starts in Pos. 3, but can end in various ways, as explained in the following text.

It is frequently found allied with other rudiments, some of which we have not yet studied, but which are mentioned below. This very interesting and useful rudiment should be thoroughly mastered. It will pay high dividends as a very practical effect in many branches of drumming.

When practicing it, say *"I—am—going—to—play—it—RIGHT"*.

Note that this rudiment *always starts with the left hand, and ends with the right*. To perfect the Seven Stroke Roll, let us review the Four Stroke Roll, the Fourth Rudiment:

The Four Stroke Roll is written: SLOW

FAST

It is a series of Singles, LRL R.

If we take a group of Four Singles:

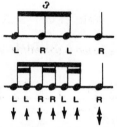

and double each Single except the last,
we produce a Seven Stroke Roll:

The hand motions of the Seven Stroke Roll are *down—up—down—up—down—up—full,* unless entering another rudiment. Sometimes a drummer is forced to decide whether he should use a Five Stroke Roll or a Seven Stroke Roll, because the notation for these two is similar. A good rule to follow in such a case is to use Fives if the tempo is fast, but to use Sevens if slow.

Also, use Fives in $\frac{6}{8}$ and Sevens in $\frac{2}{4}$. Sometimes composers carelessly use a wavy line, line as in or "Tr," meaning Trill or Roll, as in . The proper performance of the ro is then best left to the discretion of the conductor.

The Seven Stroke Roll, as previously noted, starts in Position 3, but can end in various ways. These are neither exceptions to a rule, nor are they themselves iron clad rules, but follow a logical course. A little observation on the part of the student, in the following examples, will be self-explanatory when compared with the rudiments to which they refer.

A Seven starts in Position 3, but may end in:

(1) Position 3, if followed by another roll:

(2) Position 2, if followed by a Flam (15th Rudiment):

(3) Position 4, if followed by a Drag (23rd Rudiment):

(4) Position 4, if followed by Paradiddles or Singles:

Position 3

Position 2

Right Hand DOWN
Left Hand UP

Position 4

Both Hands DOWN
(Reverse of position 3)

The Seven is sometimes written

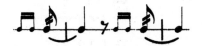

which indicates a Seven, not a Five.

Practice the following:

SEVEN STROKE EXERCISE

THE SEVEN STROKE ROLL

THE EIGHT STROKE ROLL

RUDIMENT H
The Eighth Rudiment

This rudiment is simply a Seven Stroke Roll followed by a left stroke. Like the Seven Stroke Roll, it always starts with the left hand but has an additional stroke on the end. The extra stroke is a Left Hand Stroke, which makes it the Eight Stroke Roll. Neither Ashworth nor Strube showed this rudiment, although Bruce did mention it (1862). It does not reverse, but practicing from hand to hand makes a fine exercise.

It is written:

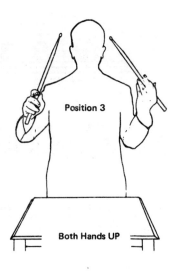

Note the two accents on end of roll, for it is

A Seven *plus one:*

(It will be noted here that three Doubles and two Singles give us the same effect.)

An example of the effective use of the Single Stroke Roll is in a Shiver, which is a rapid alternation of Singles. Here is an example of an Eight Stroke Roll followed by a Shiver, a *Seven Stroke Single:*

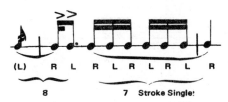

Practice the following exercises.

DON'T WAIT TO PLAY THE EIGHT, IT'S NOT 7 – 8, BUT 7 8.

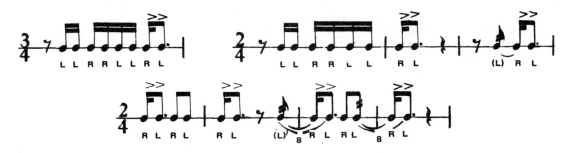

THE EIGHT STROKE ROLL

Including review of first 7 rudiments.

THE NINE STROKE ROLL

RUDIMENT I
The Ninth Rudiment

The Nine Stroke Roll is written:

It starts and ends in Position 3, and is played:

Position 3

R R L L R R L L   R   L L R R L L R R   L   R R L L R R L L   R

If we double the Single Stroke Five:

R   L   R   L   R   L   R   L   R   L

we produce the Nine Stroke Roll:

R R L L R R L L   R   L L R R L L R R   L

When practicing, say: *FOUR, EIGHT, NINE; FOUR, EIGHT, NINE.*

Accent the last stroke, and bring it to starting position.

Observe the following:

    a—It reverses.

    b—It starts and ends in Position 3.

    c—If only one Nine Stroke Roll is required, give preference to the Right Hand Nine.

    d—If it is followed by another rudiment, end it in the starting position of the new rudiment.

    e—Since Nines reverse, each hand will get an equal share of work, and thus disclose any flaws in the player's control.

Here are examples of Nine Stroke Rolls.

Two Nines, followed by Two Double Paradiddles:

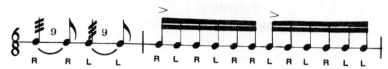

A Nine entering Paradiddles:

EXERCISES

FAST STREET BEAT

THE NINE STROKE ROLL

Single Nine

THE TEN STROKE ROLL

RUDIMENT J
The Tenth Rudiment

The Ten Stroke Roll is a Left Hand Nine followed by a fast Right Hand Single Stroke. It is equivalent to four Doubles plus two Singles.

It starts and ends in Position 3.

It is written:

It is played:

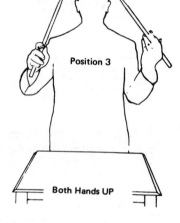

Position 3

Both Hands UP

In executing the Ten Stroke Roll it is necessary to

play the last *without the least hesitation.*

The Ten can be played Reversed, but the general rule is to play it left to right.

Rudimental drummers execute Tens with machine-like precision. Dance drummers use their rudimental training in improvisations like the following:

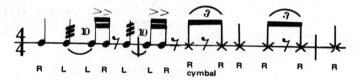

Here is an example of three Nines followed by a Ten:

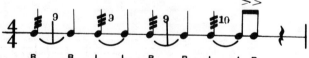

Other examples:

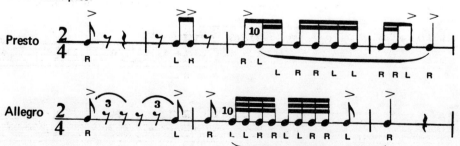

THE TEN STROKE ROLL

THE ELEVEN STROKE ROLL

RUDIMENT K
The Eleventh Rudiment

This rudiment starts and ends in Position 3.

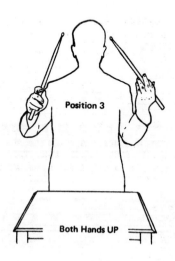

Position 3

Both Hands UP

It is written:

Notice that it ends on a quarter-note. The Nine is written to end on an eighth-note.

This rudiment does not reverse. It *reverts* — it is played *one way:*

Since writers are not consistent in their notation, it is up to the drummer to do what he deems best suited to the piece being played. If the tempo is slow, Elevens may be used; if it is lively, Nines. Good judgment and taste should be exercised. The Eleven Stroke Roll is sometimes seen as:

which demonstrates conclusively that an Eleven is required.

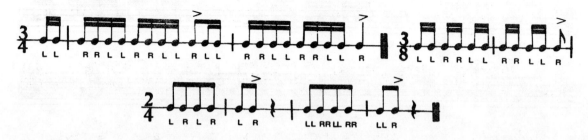

THE ELEVEN STROKE ROLL

THE THIRTEEN STROKE ROLL

RUDIMENT L
The Twelfth Rudiment

The Thirteen Stroke Roll starts and ends in Position 3.
It is written:

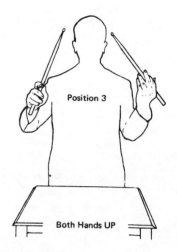

Position 3

Both Hands UP

It reverses, and is therefore playable hand to hand.

It is played:

Note the following: (a) As a left hand Thirteen, it will have four left hand motions.

As a right hand Thirteen, it will have four right hand motions.

(b) It is closely related to Fives, Nines (and Seventeens).

The Thirteen is a difficult rudiment. I have judged many individual contests and have seen one contestant after another falter when gradually closing and opening this rudiment. They invariably start playing Nines instead of Thirteens, and once they go into Nines, it is almost impossible to come out of it. Practice slowly at first, and let speed come by itself.

Here is an example of two Triple Paradiddles and two Thirteens:

R L R L R L R R   L R L R L R L L   R R L L R R L L R   R L L R   L L R R L L   R R L L R R L

A SHORT EXERCISE

R L R L   R L R   L R L R   L R L   R R L L R R L L   R R L L   R   L L R R L L R R   L L R R   L

R R R R   L L L L   R R L L R R L L R R L L   R   L L R R L L R R L L R R   L

48

THE THIRTEEN STROKE ROLL

THE FIFTEEN STROKE ROLL

RUDIMENT M
The Thirteenth Rudiment

The Fifteen Stroke Roll consists of seven Doubles and one Single full stroke. It starts and ends in Position 3. It reverts — is played one way only. It is impossible to count fast enough from one to fifteen, so we say:

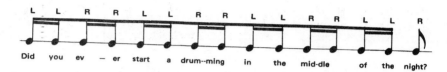

Did you ev — er start a drum--ming in the mid-dle of the night?

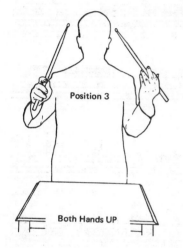

Position 3

Both Hands UP

The Fifteen is variously notated as follows:

(a)  ending with a quarter note;

(b)  ending with an eighth-note like the Thirteen;

(c)  with grace notes, and ending with a quarter note.

Some writers consider these three methods of notation correct. Here is a situation where writers use multiple ways of notating a single idea, which unfortunately does not contribute to uniformity of interpretation. The result is that drummers use their own discretion, playing the part as they deem best suited to the composition being performed.

Notice the grace notes in example (c). It seems to be preferable to the other notation, inspite of the possibility of being confused with the Seven. It may help clarify the use of grace notes and drum notation in general, if the student will study the page on REVIEW OF THE ROLLS which follows the Seventeen Stroke Roll. (It is not necessary to do this until after the Seventeen Stroke Roll has been studied.)

In cases where it is not clearly indicated whether a Thirteen or Fifteen is to be used, the drummer has only the tempo to guide him. If it is fast, a Thirteen is used, if slow, a Fifteen. This applies also to the use of Fives and Sevens when writers neglect to specify exactly what they want.

THE FIFTEEN STROKE ROLL

THE SEVENTEEN STROKE ROLL

RUDIMENT N
The Fourteenth Rudiment

The Seventeen starts and ends in Position 3.

It is written:

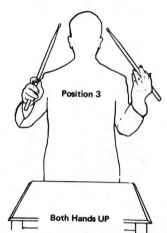

Position 3

Both Hands UP

It is played:

```
R R L L  R  R R L L   R R L L   R  R L L      R
OR L L  R  R R L L   L R R  L L  R R L L R R    L
```

It reverses, and has either five right-hand motions or five left-hand motions, as can be seen from the above.

Since it can be started right or left, bear in mind that it ends on the starting hand. When only one Seventeen is to be played, give preference to the right-hand start. Any roll following a Seventeen should be reversed. The explanation for this can be seen from the following:

```
R    R L L R      R      R    R L L
```

In England this rudiment is called Three Pace Roll. In a marching band it is executed in three steps forward:

```
1   2   3
```

In an orchestra or concert band it is directed by the conductor by three down-beats of the baton or hand.

EXERCISE

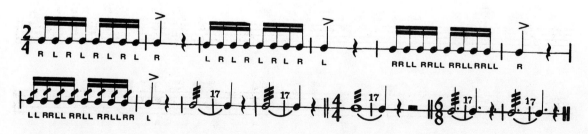

```
R L R L R L R L   R        L R L R L R L R   L        R R L L  R R L L  R R L L R R L L    R
LL R R L L  R R L L  R R L L R R    L
```

THE SEVENTEEN STROKE ROLL

REVIEW OF THE ROLL GROUP

One of the best ways of mastering a subject is to resort to frequent reviews of work already done. Techniques and conceptions that once seemed clear as crystal but which were actually grasped superficially will make themselves known. It is a surprisingly good method for evaluating one's progress and for overcoming little flaws and weak spots.

The following short summary of the Rolls, although not studied in the text as explained below, should be helpful in establishing them more firmly and will help to bring about better performance.

The Rolls may be subdivided into 5 Natural Rolls, 3 Prefixed Rolls, and 3 Augmented Rolls.

NATURAL ROLLS are those originating from Singles or Doubles. They do not have any ornamentation "fore" or "aft" attached to the "basic" pattern. These are the Four, Five, Nine, Thirteen and Seventeen.

PREFIXED ROLLS are PRODUCED when a roll is prefixed by two notes, such as a Thirteen being changed into a Fifteen by being prefixed by two notes. The Prefixed Rolls are the Seven, Eleven and Fifteen. The addition is "fore."

AUGMENTED ROLLS are those PRODUCED by adding one note at the end of roll, such as a Five being changed into a Six by the addition of one note. The Augmented Rolls are the Six, Eight and Ten.

If the Rolls are reviewed with the above in mind, it will be seen that the Natural Rolls very nearly form a basis for the others.

Singles and Doubles may also be considered Natural Rolls, and a recapitulation reveals the following:

NATURAL ROLLS: Singles, Doubles, Four, Five, Nine, Thirteen, Seventeen.

PREFIXED ROLLS: Seven, Eleven, Fifteen.

AUGMENTED ROLLS: Six, Eight, Ten.   TOTAL: 13 rudiments.

The Single Stroke Four is a Natural Roll:

The Five Stroke Roll is a Natural Roll:

The Six Stroke Roll is an Augmented Roll, since it is a Five with an added stroke:

The Seven Stroke Roll is a Prefixed Roll, since it is a (Natural) Five preceded by two notes:

The Eight Stroke Roll is an Augmented Roll, being a Seven with one additional note:

The Nine Stroke Roll is a Natural Roll:

The Ten Stroke Roll is an Augmented Roll, being a (Natural) Nine with one added note:

The Eleven Stroke Roll is a Prefixed Roll, being a (Natural) Nine with 2 prefixed notes:

The Thirteen Stroke Roll is a Natural Roll:

The Fifteen Stroke Roll is a Prefixed Roll, being a (Natural) Thirteen with 2 prefixed notes:

The Seventeen Stroke Roll is a Natural Roll:

SIX COMMON ROLLS

THE FLAM GROUP

This group consists of seven rudiments. All are derived from the first three rudiments, A — Singles, B — Doubles, C — Combinations. Either A, B, or C may be found in the *Flams*.

These Flams are:

RUDIMENT	WRITTEN & PLAYED
15 Flam	
16 Flam Tap	
17 Flam Doublet	
18 Flam Accent	
19 Flamacue	
20 Flam Paradiddle (Flamadiddle)	
21 Flamadiddle Diddle	

THE FLAM

RUDIMENT O
The Fifteenth Rudiment

A Flam is an upstroke followed immediately by a downstroke. the downstroke coming a little after the up-stroke. It should remind you of full-am. The two sounds should be clearly discernible. Rudimental drummers should be especially careful in executing this rudiment. In a rudimental contest, if the two notes are struck together, like taps or strokes with both hands, the judges will mark them down as flat handed flams. Dance drummers (and some concert drummers, too) often become very careless about this rudiment, and when criticized, will stubbornly insist they played it correctly. It is regrettable that this error of striking both notes at the same time is generally accepted by many drummers. Unfortunately, many directors of orchestras and other organizations do not understand the true character of the Flam, and so it remains uncorrected.

The Flam is written, usually, as a quarter note preceded by a small eighth note, its ornament. This small note, *grace note,* tells us whether we are to play a closed flam (fast) or an open flam (slow). The closed flam is designated by an acciaccatura (a-tshe-ak-ka-*too*-ra), the grace note with the line through it. It gets as little time as possible, and no accent, but we must still hear two notes.

Closed or short Flam:

Open or slow Flam is indicated by an appoggiatura (a-pod-je-a-*too*-ra), a "long" grace note, written without a line through it.

Open or slow Flam:

There are two kinds of Flam, the right-hand, and the left-hand. The high hand determines whether it is a right-hand or left-hand Flam.

The Positions of the sticks are, therefore, Position 1 for right-hand Flam. and Position 2 for the left-hand Flam:

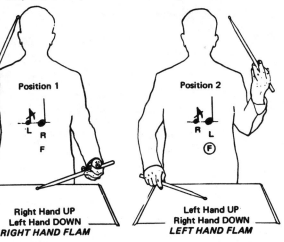

Position 1	Position 2
Right Hand UP	Left Hand UP
Left Hand DOWN	Right Hand DOWN
RIGHT HAND FLAM	*LEFT HAND FLAM*

Flams are usually played closed unless the composition is in a Maestoso, or similar mood (majestic, stately, dignified), or about metronome 100.

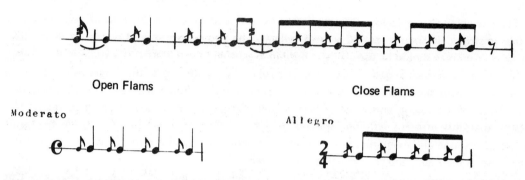

Open Flams   Close Flams

NOTE: The FLAM FIVE STROKE mentioned on page 36 will be clarified by this discussion of Flams.

EXERCISES TO DEVELOP FLAMS

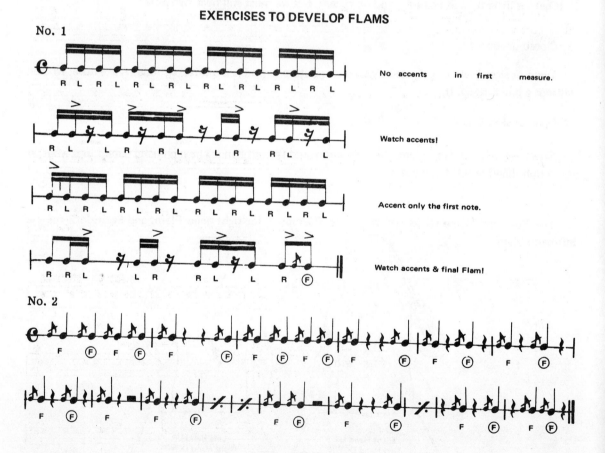

THE FLAM

THE FLAM TAP

RUDIMENT P
The Sixteenth Rudiment

The Flam Tap is a Flam followed by a tap. It can be a right hand Flam followed by a right tap, or a left-hand Flam followed by a left tap.

It is usually written:

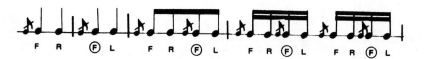

but, depending upon the tempo, it may appear as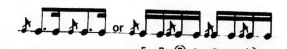

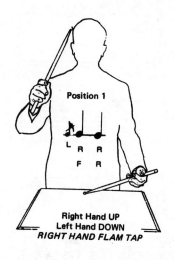

Position 1

Right Hand UP
Left Hand DOWN
RIGHT HAND FLAM TAP

There is no accent in the Flam Tap, the Flam and the Tap being of the same degree of force.

Note the positions for starting and ending, as shown in the accompanying sketches.

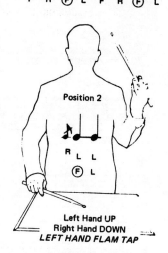

Position 2

Left Hand UP
Right Hand DOWN
LEFT HAND FLAM TAP

Some drummers mistakenly call this ♩ a Flam Accent No. 2 (another

rudiment) but it is merely a Flam Tap in 6/8 meter.

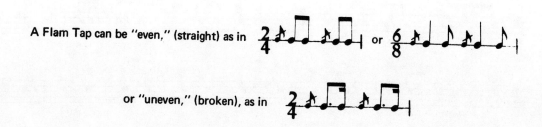

A Flam Tap can be "even," (straight) as in ♩ or ♩

or "uneven," (broken), as in ♩

60

In France a Flam is called Fla. A Flam Tap is called Fla Saute, which means a Jumping Flam. A French drummer aptly described a Flam Tap as a Flam in a hot frying pan, jumping up and down from the heat.

The Flam Tap can be done in contrary order which makes it a Tap Flam!

This contrary order is encountered frequently, and Flams may even be marked with accents, such as

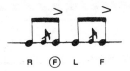

When practicing this rudiment, say Fl-am-Tap, Fl-am-Tap, and think it, and you will play a Flam Tap.

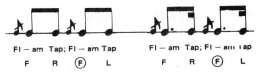

EXERCISE

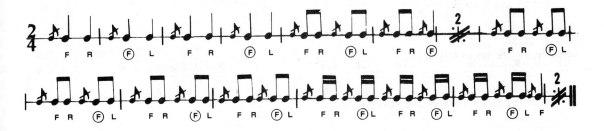

THE FLAM TAP

THE FLAM DOUBLET

RUDIMENT Q
The Seventeenth Rudiment

A Flam Doublet is a Flam followed by a Double.

It is written:

F R R   (F) L L

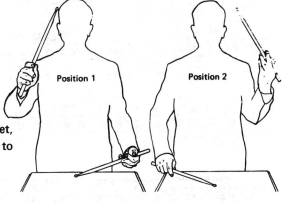

Position 1   Position 2

It starts in Position 1 and ends in Position 2.

The Flam does not lose its identity in the Flam Doublet, since the hand motions are the same as playing hand to hand Flams:

L R   R L   L R   R R   R L   L L

Although not mentioned in early drum books, the Flam Doublet takes its place as a rudiment, for it is logical that a Flam Tap can evolve quite naturally into a Flam Tap Tap, which is a Flam followed by a Double. It is used quite often in concert works.

F R   (F) L   F R R   (F) L L

EXERCISE

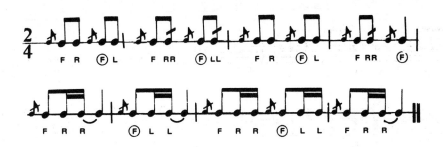

F R   (F) L   F RR   (F) LL   F R   (F) L   F RR   (F)

F R R   (F) L L   F R R   (F) L L   F R R

THE FLAM DOUBLETS

THE FLAM ACCENT

RUDIMENT R
The Eighteenth Rudiment

This rudiment consists of two Flams (or more) with interspersed notes between them, as in the following example:

F L R (F) R L   F L R (F) R L

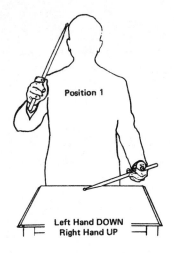

Position 1

Left Hand DOWN
Right Hand UP

The first is a right-hand Flam Accent, the second is a left-hand Flam Accent. The Flam loses its identity in this rudiment, since the three notes are played before the hands assume the opposite position. The right-hand Flam Accent starts in Position 1 and ends in Position 2, the left-hand Flam Accent vice versa.

When practicing, say:

F ↑ T   F ↑ T
Fl—am Up Tap; Fl—am Up Tap.

Make it sound happy, joyful. When playing Flam Accents the motions are not the same as in a Flam. The Flam is played as a combination tap and down-stroke, not as an up-stroke followed by a down-stroke. Both hands are therefore down after the Flam first beat.

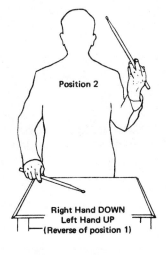

Position 2

Right Hand DOWN
Left Hand UP
(Reverse of position 1)

What follows is An Up-stroke and a Tap. This brings the sticks back to the correct starting position.

Practice the following studies before proceeding to the "Variations of Flam Accents."

EXERCISE

F L R (F) R L   F (F) R L   F L R (F) R L   F L R   (F)

Here are Singles and Doubles developed into Flam Taps and Flam Accents. Note there are NO ACCENTS in No. I, which is a good "steady drive" in a dance band. Play it uniformly soft or moderately loud throughout.

No. II has Flam Taps and Flam Accents instead of the Singles and Doubles of No. I. It is a good drum-section number to take a drum corps out to the center of a field.

THE ALL AMERICAN

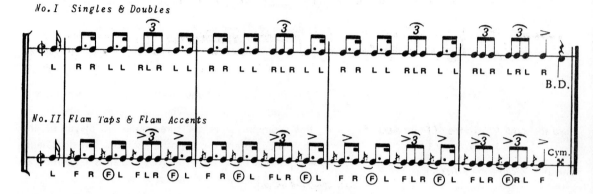

TWIRL THAT BATON

HOLD THAT PHONE

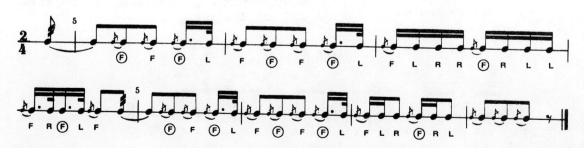

66

THE STROLLER

Here are some Variations of Flam Accents.

This is a Reverse Flam Accent:

This is an Inside Flam Accent:

This is a Hidden Flam Accent:

Here is Flam Accent sticking, but not true Flam Accent rhythm:

THE FLAM ACCENT

THE FLAMACUE

RUDIMENTS
The Nineteenth Rudiment

This rudiment is written

It has only one accent, and does not reverse. In practicing, say

It's A Flam-a- cue, march-ING down the street!

In order to perfect this rudiment, be sure to observe the following:

a — Start in a sort of "half" Position 1, with the right hand not as high as usual, half way between a Tap and a Stroke.

b — Pronounce the words with the accent on "A" and "CHING." Although these verbal accents do not fall on the natural accents of the word syllables, it is precisely this kind of stimulating "obstacle course" that develops accuracy and excellent coordination between mind and sticks.

c — Be sure to LIFT THAT RIGHT HAND on the last note "street."

d — The second Flam loses its natural motion and becomes a Tap, Full-Stroke.

Although several Flamacues may be repeated, they are all played with the same sticking:

The Flamacue following the Flam Doublet:

A single Flam following a Flamacue:

There is also this figure described as a Double Flamacue:

Flocton called two fast Flam Taps and a Flam a Flamapoo:

A Flamacue, a Flam added, a Flam Accent, and a left-hand Flam:

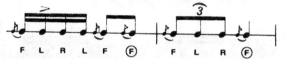

EXERCISE. *Exaggerate the accent after the Flam — an accented left Down-Stroke.*

HALF & HALF

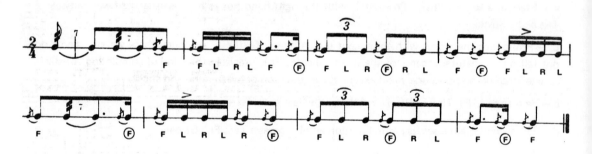

IT TAKES TWO TO FLAM

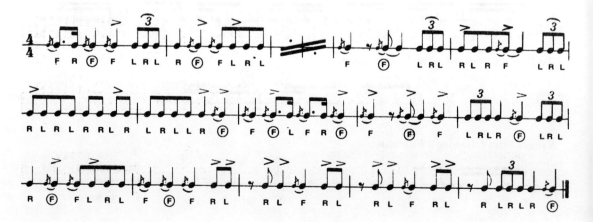

THE FLAMACUE

71

THE FLAM PARADIDDLE

RUDIMENT T
The Twentieth Rudiment

This rudiment is also called the Flamadiddle. It is written:

It is a vigorous, yet graceful rudiment. It reverses, and is executed as if playing Flams hand to hand. The Sticking is Flam, Left, Double; Flam, Right, Double. It starts in Position 1, and ends in Position 2. Accent the Flam in each repetition of the Flam Paradiddle pattern.

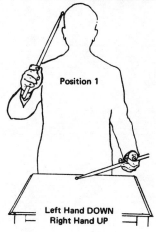

Be careful not to digress into a Flamadiddle followed by a Paradiddle, that is, *do not drop the Flam in the repetition.*

The Flam Paradiddle is a very useful rudiment. It leads into many fine combinations, especially in improvising.

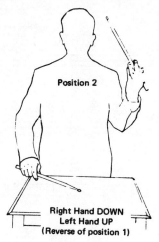

The Flam in this rudiment is not played with the complete Flam movement since the left hand on the first Flam (also the right hand on the second Flam) does not go up, but stays down to play the upstroke which follows. Be sure to observe the up and down strokes:

Flam Accents are often used with Flam Paradiddles:

72

"SARASOTA"

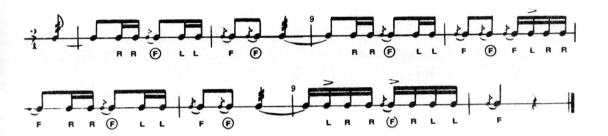

RELAX

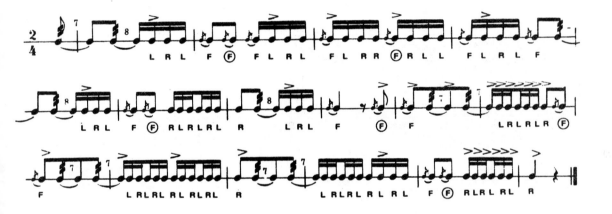

THE JAY BIRD

THE FLAM PARADIDDLE

THE FLAM PARADIDDLE DIDDLE
(Flamadiddle Diddle)

RUDIMENT U
The Twenty First Rudiment

This rudiment is of tremendous importance to every drummer. It is probably the best to study for developing stick control. The drummer that executes this rudiment with precision is well on the way to success.

It is written:

When practicing, say *Flam-a-did-dle did-dle,   Flam-a-did-dle did-dle!*

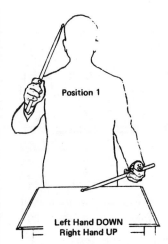

Position 1

Left Hand DOWN
Right Hand UP

It starts in Position 1, and ends in Position 2. In each pattern, the last note should be an upstroke, so that the sticks will be in position to play the Flam in the repetition of the rudiment, as it *reverses.*

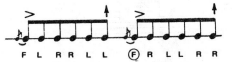

Accent on first note, Up-stroke on last note, of eacn pattern. The importance of the Up-stroke is demonstrated very well here. This rudiment develops a "lift," a good up-stroke.

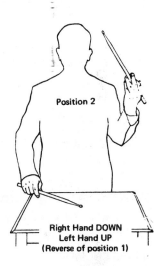

Position 2

Right Hand DOWN
Left Hand UP
(Reverse of position 1)

EXERCISE — THE FLAMADIDDLE DIDDLE

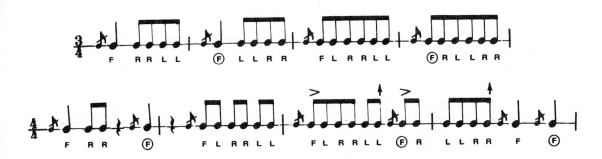

THE DUTCH

A fine rudimental study, making use of the Flam,
the Seven, the Flamacue and Flamadiddle Diddle.

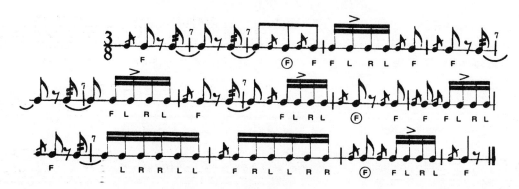

THE DECEPTIVE F.P.D.

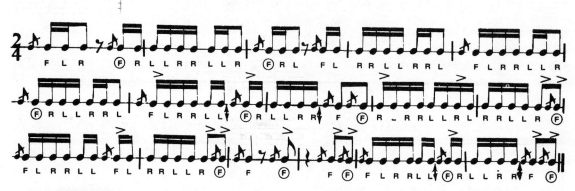

FLAM CHOWDER   A CONCOCTION OF ALL THE MEMBERS OF THE FLAM CLAN.

Flam, Flam Tap, Flam Doublet, Flam Accent,
Flamacue, Flamadiddle, Flam Paradiddle Diddle.

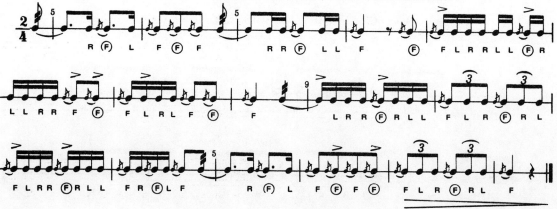

THE FLAM PARADIDDLE DIDDLE

THE RUFF GROUP

This group consists of five rudiments:

V — Ruffs and Half Drags.

W — Drags — Single, Double, Full.

X — Drag Paradiddles.

Y — Lesson 25 — The Ratamott.

Z — Ratamacues — Single, Double, Triple.

THE RUFF AND HALF DRAG

RUDIMENT V
The Twenty Second Rudiment

It is written with a double appoggiatura:

Like the Flam, the Ruff takes its name from the high hand. Since it reverses there is a right-hand and a

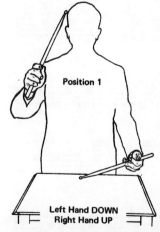

Position 1

Left Hand DOWN
Right Hand UP

left-hand Ruff. The Right-hand Ruff starts in Position 1 and ends in Position 2, the Left-hand Ruff vice versa. The motions are Tap, Up-stroke, Down-stroke:

When this rudiment is played closed, it is a Ruff, sounding like one who rolls his R's like "R-r-ruff"!

When played open and without the accent it is called a Half Drag.

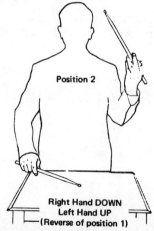

Position 2

Right Hand DOWN
Left Hand UP
(Reverse of position 1)

It is good drumming to play this rudiment as a Ruff (closed) if it is by itself, but if it is "absorbed" by another rudiment, to play it as a Half Drag (open).

The Ruff is merely the result of a Double plus a Single (Rudiment B plus Rudiment A). It has the quality of a command. It is rugged and robust, and can also be boisterous. It was not in Ashworth's book, but Bruce and Strube mentioned it.

When practicing the Ruff, say:

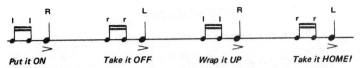

Put it ON   Take it OFF   Wrap it UP   Take it HOME!

Ruffs appear in the opening measures of the Allegro Con Fuoco movement of Dvorak's New World Symphony, and in the middle portion of Bagley's National Emblem March.

The following figure is called a Tap Ruff:

It sounds like a Half Drag, but the sticking is in single form, hand to hand. It is used a great deal in Galops, and makes a delightful effect with wire brushes in fast dance tunes. Die Fledermaus by Johann Strauss, calls for Tap Ruffs in several places.

Excerpt from DEDICATION & BENEDICTION from Meyerbeer's "Les Huguenots." (Ruffs)

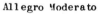

Exercise on Ruffs.

Exercise on Half Drags.

Excerpt from Rossini's "William Tell." (Ruffs)

Allegro Vivace

Exercise "The Ruffs"

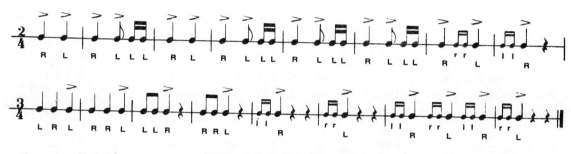

HICKORY, DICKORY, DOCK!

I. Singles & Doubles

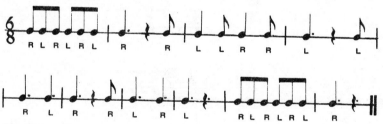

II. Flam Accents & Flam Taps.

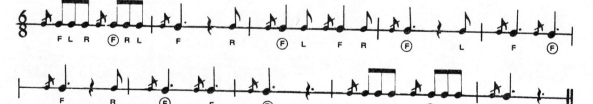

III. Five Stroke Rolls (hand to hand), Flam Accents, Reversed Flam Tap (i.e., Tap Flam), & Double Paradiddles.

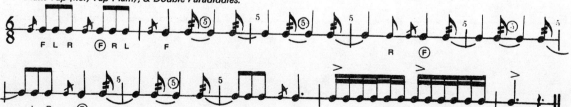

80

THE RUFF AND HALF DRAG

THE DRAGS

RUDIMENT W
The Twenty Third Rudiment

Some authorities claim the Drags are somewhat confusing. It is suggested that an examination of the development of the Drags will help to better understand them.

Under the general term Drags, there are four patterns, each distinctly characteristic, yet related to each other. The Half Drag, which was treated as an Open Ruff without accent under Rudiment 22, re-appears here as part of the Drags. This overlapping may possibly account for some of the confusion that surrounds the Drags. Yet it is not a hindrance if a relationship between the rudiments is recognized. In fact, any other classification is likely to further complicate the subject. Again, it is possible that the words Half, Single, Double, Full, when applied to the term Drag do not imply a relationship between these four Drags. (And only Single Drag and Double Drag are N.A.R.D. examination requirements!)

The following discussion attempts to clarify the Drags, but the student should first be sure he has a good knowledge of the preceding rudiments and studies.

* * * * * * * * * * * *

THE DRAGS

There are four distinct patterns embraced by the name The Drags:

1. The Half Drag, which is an Open Ruff minus the accent.

2. The Single Drag.

3. The Double Drag.

4. The Full Drag.

All Drags have a few things in common:

1 — They start in Position 4, both hands down, but may end otherwise.

2 — The first three notes are Taps.

3 — Within their patterns, there is always an Open Ruff in one form or another, but in this group it is called the Half Drag, and is played as Taps, whereas it was played differently as an Open Ruff.

4 — Their accents are of great importance, as they can alter the character of the same basic pattern that is used for all Drags.

5 — All Drags Reverse.

Under Rudiment 22, Ruffs and Half Drags, we learned that a Half Drag is an Open Ruff, minus accent. THIS IS THE POINT WHERE DRAGS BEGIN TO TAKE FORM. Before we attempt to do any playing, let us first compare the patterns of the Drags, as shown in the following analysis:

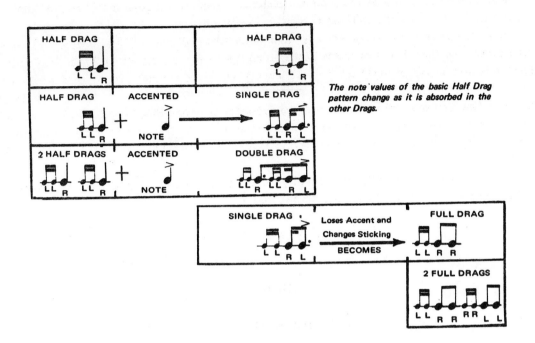

The note values of the basic Half Drag pattern change as it is absorbed in the other Drags.

From the above analysis we can draw these conclusions:

1 — Drags are derived from the figure ♩♩, which we recognize as an un-accented Ruff, or Half Drag.

♩♩ , with accent, it's a Ruff, and is played Close;

♩♩ , no accent, it's a Half Drag, is played somewhat Open, in 3 Taps.

By combining this pattern with itself or with another single note, we get all the other Drags.

2 — In the Flam, a single grace note ornaments the main note; in the Drags, two grace notes ornament the main note.

3 — The placement of the accents is important: The Single Drag and the Double Drag have accents, but the Half Drag and the Full Drag have no accents.

4 — The sticking for the Full Drag is similar to the Flam Tap:

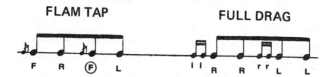

FLAM TAP

F   R   (F)   L

FULL DRAG

l l   R   R   r r L   L

Notice that each note has the same degree of force — no accents.

5 — The sticking and the accents make the difference between a Single Drag and a

Full Drag: 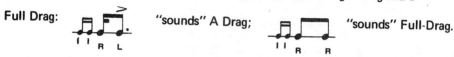 "sounds" A Drag; "sounds" Full-Drag.

l l   R   L   l l   R   R

THE SINGLE DRAG

The Single Drag is basically  a Half Drag plus an accented note.

The sticking is 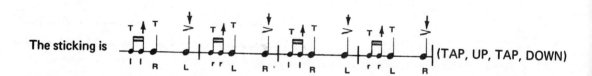 (TAP, UP, TAP, DOWN)

l l R   L   r r L   R   l l R   L   r r L   R

"Straight" $\frac{2}{4}$

R l l R L r r L   R l l R L r r L

"Choppy" $\frac{2}{4}$

R l l R L r r L   R l l R L r r L

Start in Position 1. The high hand comes down and stays down. How Drags end, depends on what follows. In the Single Drag, however, the hand motions are as indicated above because the second left had to go up in order to come down accented on the fourth note.

84

SINGLE DRAG STUDIES

Watch accents. Repeat Indefinitely.

Compare this study in 6/8 *with the next one in* 2/4

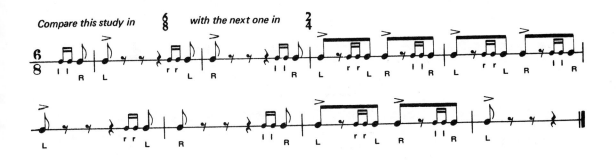

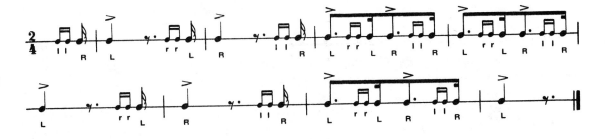

I'LL BUY THAT!

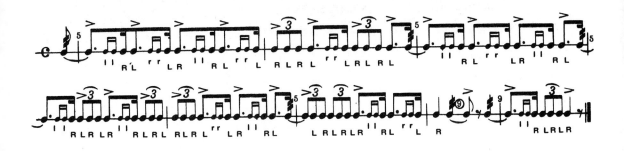

HEY! HEY!

Five Stroke Roll ON THE BEAT in measures 1 & 5.

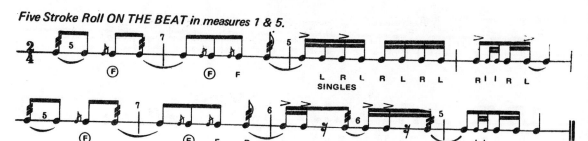

EVOLUTION OF THE SINGLE DRAG

THE DOUBLE DRAG

The Double Drag is basically

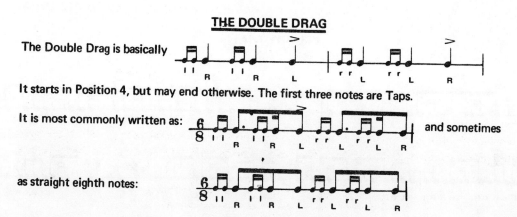

It starts in Position 4, but may end otherwise. The first three notes are Taps.

It is most commonly written as:

and sometimes

as straight eighth notes:

Notice that the note values of the basic pattern change in $\frac{6}{8}$, but the sticking remains UNCHANGED

ON DOUBLE DRAGS

PLAYED 2 BEATS TO A MEASURE ("IN 2")

THE FULL DRAG

The Full Drag is basically

It starts in Position 4, but may end otherwise. The first three notes are definitely Taps. The authentic manner of performing the entire Full Drag is with all Taps, although it is not always done that way. The discerning and ambitious drummer, however will make it a point to master it that way as well as doing only the first three notes as Taps.

The hand motions of the Full Drag are similar to that of the Flam Tap, and there are no accents, all notes being played with the same degree of force.

FLAM TAP   FULL DRAG

Sometimes Full Drags are written in an unorthodox manner for a special effect, in which the hands perform graceful gymnastic movements. In this case, the notes are heavily accented and Strokes can be used:

The Full Drag is well represented in Smetana's The Bartered Bride Overture; other Drags are found in The Slow Scotch, Dawning of the Day, Breakfast Call, Dinner Call.

When practicing the Drags, it is well to review pages 82 and 83, observing the similarities and differences described in those pages.

A thumb-nail summary of the Drags:

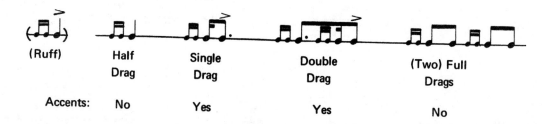

(Ruff)	Half Drag	Single Drag	Double Drag	(Two) Full Drags
Accents:	No	Yes	Yes	No

EXERCISES

I.

II.

NO ACCENTS. ALL TAPS — WRIST ONLY.

III.

ALL ACCENTS.   ARM AND WRIST.

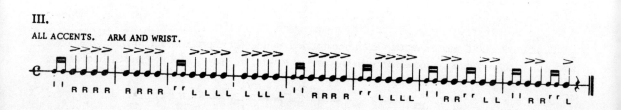

THE DRAGS

THE DRAG PARADIDDLES

RUDIMENT X
The Twenty Fourth Rudiment

Bruce described Drag Paradiddles as follows:

Drag Paradiddle No. 1:

Drag Paradiddle No. 2:

Strube differed, and gave the following version, which is the one adopted by the National Association of Rudimental Drummers:

Drag Paradiddle No. 1:

Drag Paradiddle No. 2:

In Sousa's book his drummer described a Drag Paradiddle as:

and gave the name Stroke and Drag Paradiddle to:

Moeller (1925) described all these variations simply as five exercises on drag paradiddles.

From the above data, it appears that we have a group of closely related rudiments that may be placed under one main heading of Drag Paradiddles.

In the opinion of this writer, Drag Paradiddles are best represented by the choice of the N.A.R.D. of Strube's Paradiddles No. 1 and No. 2.

By the simple process of comparing their similarities and differences, we can see their evolution from a drag and a paradiddle, and learn to better recognize and perform them!

A comparison of the Drag Paradiddles shows the following similarities and differences:

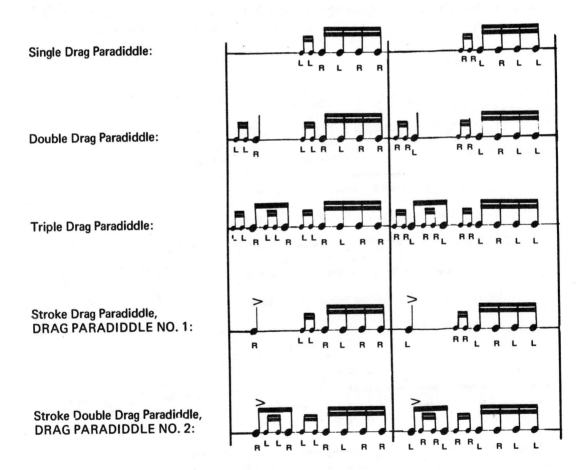

Single Drag Paradiddle:

Double Drag Paradiddle:

Triple Drag Paradiddle:

Stroke Drag Paradiddle,
DRAG PARADIDDLE NO. 1:

Stroke Double Drag Paradiddle,
DRAG PARADIDDLE NO. 2:

The foregoing shows a variety of Drag Paradiddles. For the sake of simplicity, a detailed discussion of each one is not necessary, and only the two forms adoped by the N.A.R.D. will be described. These are the Drag Paradiddle No. 1, and the Drag Paradiddle No. 2.

THE DRAG PARADIDDLE No. 1

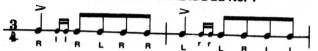

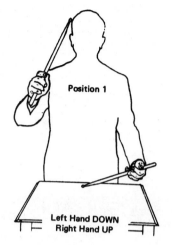

Position 1

Left Hand DOWN
Right Hand UP

It starts in Position 1, with the sticking as indicated, then goes into Position 2 at the two right hand Taps. For the repetition, the sticking is reversed, starting with a left hand Down Stroke.

THE DRAG PARADIDDLE No. 2

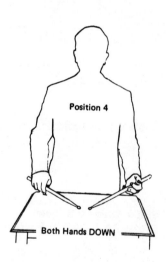

Position 4

Both Hands DOWN

It starts in Position 1, with the sticking as indicated, then goes into Position 4; Half Drag commencing with the left; another Half Drag commencing with left; a left Up-Stroke, and two right Taps. For the repetition, the sticking is reversed.

EXERCISES

THE DRAG PARADIDDLES

THE RATAMOTT

RUDIMENT Y
The Twenty Fifth Rudiment

Editor's Note: For a long time this rudiment has been nameless. It has been referred to as "the twenty five," "number 25," or as "Lesson 25." It is not clear why this valuable rudiment should be nameless like an unwanted poor relation, which it is not. It occurred to this editor, that in recognition of Vincent L. Mott's contributions to the art of drumming the name Ratamott would be a fitting testimonial to a deserving teacher and musician, and quite appropriate to the nature of the rudiment. It is hoped this suggestion will not be construed as presumptuous on the part of this editor, but merely as a gesture of acknowledgment of the work of Vincent L. Mott in advancing the art of drumming.

This rudiment is written: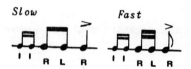

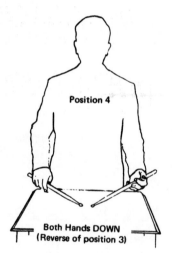

Position 4

Both Hands DOWN
(Reverse of position 3)

It starts and ends in Position 4.

From Position 4, say

Tap-Tap-UP, Tap-DOWN.

Accent only the last note; the Down Stroke gets the accent in this rudiment.

It reverts, and like the Four Stroke:

it is best played one way only:

94

For improved stick control, practice from hand to hand (reversing), but when called for in a contest, play it one way. Notice how the accent moves up in the following figures:

Be observant of the right hand Strokes: one is an Up, one is a hard Down; the Up-stroke follows the two left Taps, the Down-stroke follows the one left tap.

EVOLUTION OF THE RATAMOTT

EVERYTHING'S IN ITS PLACE

THE RATAMOTT

THE RATAMACUES

RUDIMENT Z
The Twenty Sixth Rudiment

There are three Ratamacues, the Single, the Double and the Triple. The basic pattern for Ratamacues is the Single Ratamacue, as seen from the following comparison:

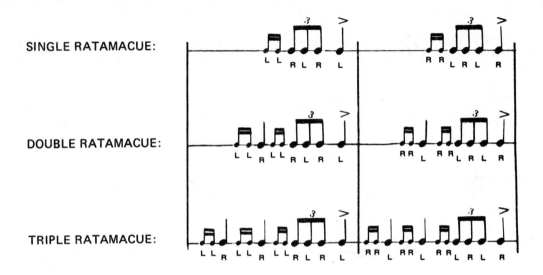

SINGLE RATAMACUE:

DOUBLE RATAMACUE:

TRIPLE RATAMACUE:

All Ratamacues start and end in Position 4, and are played from hand to hand (they reverse). The last note is always accented.

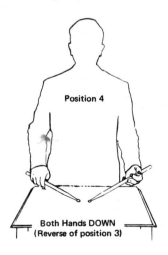

Position 4

Both Hands DOWN
(Reverse of position 3)

Note how well Single Ratamacues fit in with Single Drags:

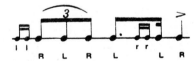

Ratamacues are well represented in Tschaikovsky's March Slav and Overture 1812, Liszt's Hungarian Rhapsodie No. 2, in many orchestral arrangements by Leroy Anderson and Morton Gould. Drummers in dance bands use Ratamacues to excellent advantage. It is a very effective and useful rudiment.

THE SINGLE RATAMACUE

The Single Ratamacue is:

Observe the sticking and the hand motions. The last note is always accented. This is the basic pattern of the Double Ratamacue and the Triple Ratamacue. It should therefore be mastered before going on to the others.

Accents may be changed in Ratamacues, but for authenticity, the above is rudimentally correct.

Sometimes accents appear, and the Half Drag figure is changed to a Ruff:

The Single Ratamacue

THE DOUBLE RATAMACUE

The Double Ratamacue is:

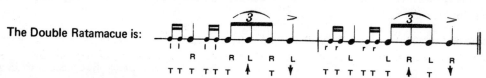

Observe the sticking and the hand motions. Notice that ONE Half Drag precedes the Single Ratamacue to make a Double Ratamacue.

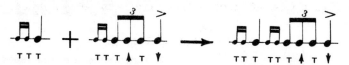

The Double Ratamacue

THE TRIPLE RATAMACUE

The Triple Ratamacue is:

Observe the hand motions and notice that TWO Half Drags precede a Single Ratamacue to make a Triple Ratamacue.

The Triple Ratamacue

DON'T FLUFF THAT RUFF!

WELL, WELL, IT'S W.F.L.!

THE RATAMACUES

STUDIES

Students will find the following studies of value in acquiring polish and increased mastery. Practice these until they can be played fluently and with utmost clarity. At first, do not practice at fast tempos. Strive only for clearness and accuracy, letting speed come by itself.

REPEAT EACH STUDY SEVERAL TIMES.

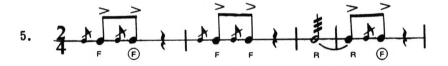

**Four rudiments in a short exercise: Flam Tap, Flam
Doublet and Flamadiddle, ending with a Flam.**

7.

8.
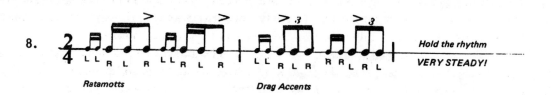

Ratamotts *Drag Accents*

Hold the rhythm
VERY STEADY!

Two short exercises to improve hand motions. Carefully observe the down and up motions on the following Singles. Each measure is Down, Tap, Tap, Up — Down, Tap, Tap, Up, back to back. Be sure to observe the back to back sticking of R L R L, L R L R. These two short studies, No. 9 and No. 10, make excellent warm up exercises, and develop form and style by stressing the Down and Up-Strokes and the Taps. Place the accents on the Down-Strokes. Practice No. 9 until some facility is acquired before proceeding to No. 10.

9.

KEEP
REPEATING

Now change the rhythm and note the difference. Use the same hand motions.

10.
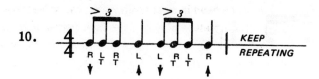

KEEP
REPEATING